to dam & Helen

love

Pierre

County Cavan

—Land of Water, Earth and Air—

Text by Ciaran Parker

Paintings by Jim Mc Partlin

Cottage
Publications

First published by Cottage Publications,
an imprint of Laurel Cottage Ltd.
Donaghadee, N. Ireland 2008.
Copyrights Reserved.
© Illustrations by Jim Mc Partlin 2008.
© Text by Ciaran Parker 2008.
All rights reserved.
No part of this book may be reproduced or stored on any media
without the express written permission of the publishers.
Design & origination in Northern Ireland.
Printed & bound in China.
ISBN 978 1 900935 67 8

The Author

Ciaran Parker is a historian, writer and researcher. He studied history at Trinity College Dublin, earning a PhD for a thesis on the politics and society of Co. Waterford in the late medieval period. He has lectured in T.C.D. and University College, Dublin and has contributed numerous articles to a wide range of publications on medieval social history. He is also interested in the economic and cultural life of the South Ulster area over the past four centuries. Since October 2006 Ciaran has written a weekly column for the *Cavan Echo* newspaper entitled 'Echoes of the Past' which aims to highlight under-appreciated aspects of local history, as well as presenting others from a different perspective.

Ciaran is also keenly interested in international business and development economics and has written several books and articles on business topics and strategic management, some of which have been translated into Russian, Chinese, and Korean.

The Artist

Jim Mc Partlin hails from Dublin, but has been living in Virginia, Co. Cavan since 2004. He has spent most of his working life as a Graphic Designer but has always had a passion for drawing and painting and started exhibiting in Dublin nearly 20 years ago.

Since moving to Cavan, Jim has been working as a full-time artist. The local landscape has provided the inspiration for much of his painting. His yearly watercolour exhibitions at the Ramor Theatre in Virginia have proved very popular and his work has been bought by Cavan County Council, Meath County Council and Virginia's College and Credit Union.

Working on the series of paintings for this book has given Jim a huge appreciation of the varied topography and culture of County Cavan and he hopes that the reader, be they from Cavan or beyond, will be encouraged to look again and linger in one of Ireland's most beautiful counties.

Contents

County Cavan: An Introduction

The landscape of County Cavan is dominated by three elements: water, earth and air. Certainly the first of these is the most important. It is said that there are three hundred and sixty-five lakes in Cavan – one for every day of the year and in a leap year we simply dig a hole, for the water-table is so high and the ground so permeated by water that any hollow will soon fill. But, as anyone who has ever visited Cavan will know, it is not a soggy morass, and the three elements mentioned above combine in the most beautiful poetry to form landscapes of mesmerising and haunting beauty.

It is impossible to think about Cavan without thinking about water. There are some locations near Cootehill and Maudabawn in the north-east of the county where it is said

land is not measured by the acre but by the gallon. Some tourist promoters call Cavan 'The Lakeland County', but this rather twee label entirely misses the point. A lot of the most beautiful waterscapes in Cavan have nothing to do with lakes, and, furthermore, there are different types of lakes here. There are innumerable small lakes, usually clogged with reeds providing nesting grounds for ducks. Then there are the larger expanses of water, like Loughs Ramor, Sillane, Sheelin and MacNean. Legends are told about how they were formed. For example, it is said that Lough Sillane was formed when a heedless young girl forgot to replace the lid on a well which subsequently overflowed. Their banks have been inhabited for millennia by those seeking the rich harvest of fish from their waters. There were those who sought safety on islands in these lakes, believing (sometimes inaccurately) that the lakes' waters offered protection against marauders and raiders. Sometimes these island retreats were man-made crannogs, accessible by flimsy boats or semi-invisible track-ways of stones. Lakes were places of danger for the careless, as discovered by the party of schoolchildren who perished with their teacher on Lough Sillane in 1878, or the funeral cortege to Lough Sheelin's Church Island who fell through the ice to a chilly grave.

The central part of Co. Cavan is dominated by Upper Lough Erne. When viewed on a map, or from a satellite, it appears like a tangled web of inter-connecting lakes and waterways. For the visitor travelling along its banks for the first time it is often hard to believe that it is one single lake. The sailor who travels along its length enjoys a kaleidoscope of vistas, some hedged in by trees, others of placid water flowing between meadows. This has long been a means of entry into the heart of Cavan, employed by some of the region's earliest inhabitants who left evidence of their habitation such as at Killykeen. Later travellers included monks like St Mogue, the founder of the monastery at Drumlane, as well as those who built the area's first cathedral on Trinity Island in Lough Oughter, the original site of the Romanesque doorway which is now to be found at Kilmore.

The Erne was passable at only certain locations, such as Belturbet, and when Cavan was visited in the early thirteenth century the Anglo Normans ensured control of the river by building a fort on Turbot Island near Belturbet and a more substantial stone structure at Clough Oughter. In 1369, a coup d'etat against the chieftain of the O'Reillys was thwarted when the ruler of Fermanagh sent a flotilla of support down the river Erne. At a later date excursionists from Cavan's leisured classes kept sailing boats on its waters, while others built charming summer cottages at places like Killykeen.

Medieval geographers believed that Ireland was divided by one great river, in other words that the Shannon and the Erne were joined. We now know they are two separate river systems. The idea of joining them by a canal obsessed many minds in the late eighteenth century and finally it was decided in 1839 that a canal would be built from the Erne near Belturbet to the Shannon in Co. Leitrim. Work on this bold engineering project began in 1856 and after over six years of work it was completed. However, the expected commercial volume failed spectacularly to materialise and it ended up being one of the most expensive drainage ditches in history, as the drainage of the lands through which it passed was one of the few long-lasting legacies of its construction.

Travel along the length of the Erne was for many years performed by Erne cots. These were small, flat-bottomed, keel-less boats, traditionally made from larch-wood which was both light and water-resistant. They were used for transporting people to market and church services, as well as children to school. Cots were used for ferrying funeral corteges, and they were also useful for ferrying cattle to islands in the lake. But the Erne was a dangerous water-way, and a turn from an otherwise placid piece of water around an inconspicuous headland might bring boat and passengers into uncontrollable currents, with consequent loss of life. In 1821 no less than eighteen people drowned when a cot capsized on the River Erne.

Many of Co. Cavan's rivers drain ultimately into the Erne. One of these is the Annalee which enters the Erne just below Butlersbridge. Its fast-flowing waters were the location of Co. Cavan's first industrial revolution, as in the eighteenth century mills for processing grain and flax were built along its banks between Ballyhaise and Cootehill.

As late as the nineteenth century there were fishermen who made their living fishing from Cavan's lakes and settling their catch at local markets. This was especially true along Upper Lough Erne, but they disappeared as a result of changes in the water level caused by the drainage of Lough Erne. Anglers can still enjoy the peace and tranquillity of casting their lines into Cavan's lakes, whether for salmon, trout or coarse fish. Alas, one of Cavan, and Europe's, best trout lakes, Lough Sheelin was brought to the very verge of extinction as a result of agricultural pollution. It is making a very slow recovery.

The Erne, not to mention many of its tributaries, is embraced by wooded banks. Until about four hundred years ago much of Co. Cavan was covered in forestry. All that remains of this now are the occasional finds of bog oak or place-names containing tree elements like 'Derry', from the Irish *Doire*. These were largely cleared in the seventeenth and eighteenth century and in places were replaced by plantations of non-Irish trees in the parks of the houses of the local elite, such as at Farnham, Ballyhaise and Cormey Castle near Kingscourt. The latter with its wonderfully romantic vistas became in the late twentieth century the Dun an Ri forest park. Other forest parks, such as that at Killykeen, have helped to make the county's landscape less of a wind-blasted heath.

The soils in Cavan are in general poor and unyielding. For centuries farmers have tried to eke a livelihood from them, though with mixed success. Some crops have been historically more resilient than others.

The humble spud has filled many a belly with its carbohydrate-rich flesh, so much so that many a Cavanman (and Cavanwoman) refuses to accept the bona fide of any meal unless accompanied by the requisite 'balls of flour'. Yet potato cultivation has needed skill and equipment. The best way of growing them in such a water-logged landscape was using the lazy-bed method. There was nothing lazy about the means by which a bed was raised by turves and sods being dug out of a ditch. The depression provided drainage, while the seed potatoes were then sown in the raised part, traditionally using a narrow wooden dibber called a spalpeen or guggering-stick. They were then covered with soil and some manure, sometimes contained in a basket called a bardog carried on the back of a horse or donkey. The tool by which the ditches were dug was the loy – a long, heavy spade that was more like a hand-plough but which was perfectly suited to Cavan's heavier soils. Great pride was displayed by the man who could make his beds straight. Sadly these arts, along with potato cultivation in general, seem in decline now, as most people prefer to buy their spuds in cellophane bags.

Another crop that thrived in the soils of east and north Cavan was the flax plant. In the months of July and August it carried blooms of sky blue, yet it was not its aesthetic qualities that caused it to be grown so assiduously. The plant was harvested by being pulled out of the ground. It then went through a number of stages, including being immersed in water to cause the fibres to swell up. This was done in specially excavated flax-holes, which are still found in many parts of the county. These were deep and were hazardous for small children. What was more the inundated flax poisoned the water in which it was soaked. The end of the process was the production of yarn which could be spun into linen cloth. The heyday of flax-growing and domestic linen production was around 1800. After that the whole process fell victim to cheaper mechanisation and the availability of synthetic fabrics, but small-scale flax production continued in some areas around Cootehill and Bailieborough until the middle of the twentieth century.

The north and east of Cavan is dominated by drumlins. When seen from the air it is easy to understand the name given by geographers to such a landscape: basket-of-eggs topography, and the collective noun for a group of drumlins is not surprisingly a swarm. They were formed when the last ice sheet melted, leaving behind a myriad of low but steep-sided hills. Such a landscape can be terrifying, especially to the traveller who loses his way on a foggy night in the vicinity of Kill near Cootehill as it is almost impossible to find your way out without the use of a satellite navigation unit, since all the roads meander through a near identical landscape devoid of features other than drumlins. There are those who say that the inhabitants of drumlin areas have a marked insularity of character, as they are unable to see beyond the next drumlin.

Further west in Cavan the landscape is dominated by bog-land. This provided heat and warmth to generations of farmers, often attempting to bring up families of twelve, thirteen or more on handkerchief-sized holdings of scrub. In early summer this was often covered by a psychedelic carpet of gorse and heather. Sometimes the turves were used as a roofing material, as in the Dowra area. At one time considerable areas of west Cavan were covered with trees, but these were gradually felled, mostly to provide fuel for the iron smelting industry in Swanlinbar. In certain spots in West Cavan the trees have returned as part of managed plantations which, when seen from afar, have the appearance of infantry huddled up against the cold. They are amongst the area's few inhabitants now, along with the sheep whose bleating breaks the profound silence of West Cavan's mountains.

The last essential element in Cavan – air – is perhaps the most essential yet it is the one most easily taken for granted. It is the medium through which the birdsong from Cavan's woods and hedgerows pass and through which trickles the murmur of the county's ever-present waters. It is the *sine qua non* of the atmosphere through which we can view the county's beauty. It changes with the seasons: there is the crystal clear atmosphere of a bright summer's day, the slightly more sublimated hues of autumn, or the fog and mist which frequently clothe large segments of the county in winter. At any time of the year it is not uncommon for it to be heavily laden with the sickening fumes from some piggery or rendering plant.

County Cavan is often referred to as a Border Area. This is used to imply an inward-looking defensiveness supposedly found in areas near political frontiers. But the fact is that some parts of Co. Cavan have been border areas for thousands, maybe millions of years, as shown by the natural watershed that runs along part of the Cuilcagh ridge. Border areas are often areas of transition, whose lines of demarcation are at best fuzzy. What is certainly true is that Cavan has not been so much a border area as a borders area, where a number of cultures come into contact.

This is clearly shown by the language used for everyday communication in Cavan until comparatively recently. English has been the dominant vernacular in most of Cavan since the mid nineteenth century, but Irish remained influential. Some Irish phrases were used such as *Mar dhea; an* expression indicating that what had preceded it should not be taken too seriously. A person who was very hungry complained of having the 'fergorta' from the Irish *fear gorta,* or hungry grass, while a small cabin was called either a tiggeen (tigin) or a pruheen (proichin). A second element of local speech is provided by Ulster Scots words and phrases. These may have been introduced by Scottish planters, or through contact with parts of Ulster where Ulster Scots was the vernacular. In Cavan people in receipt of unemployment benefits were 'on the brew' and these were handed out in the 'brew office'. An infectious disease, of either humans or animals, was a trake, while lane-ways were lined with a shough. The last element comes from archaic English; there are some words used in the Cavan vernacular which would be more familiar to a seventeenth-century English speaker than to a contemporary, such as 'haveril' for an uncouth and boorish person. These may have been introduced by English planters, or they may be the result of influences emanating from Dublin and Ireland's east coast, forces which were felt keenly in the east of the county.

The pull of geography and Irish geopolitics can be seen too in the area's history. Breifne, the old tribal kingdom which preceded the formation of Co. Cavan, was traditionally viewed as part of the Irish province of Connacht. Indeed, along with Annaly (modern Co. Longford) it be-longed to what was called the *garbh-thrian Chonnachta* or 'rough third' of Connacht. Its ruling clans, including the O'Reillys, traced their ancestry back to a family originating in Co. Roscommon. During the later middle ages the eastern part of Breifne, which corresponded most closely to modern Cavan, moved into the political orbit of the chieftains of Ulster such as the O'Neills and when, in the early seventeenth century, Cavan was planted with settlers from England and Scotland it was part of a scheme of plantation affecting the whole of Ulster. Cavan has remained part of the geographical and sporting province of Ulster to this day.

But with the advent of partition in 1922 Co. Cavan (along with Donegal and Monaghan) became part of the Irish Free State and subsequently the Irish Republic. Its capital was in Dublin and it was towards this location on the east coast that the county had to look for its laws and administration.

In spite of the importance of borders, Cavan as an administrative unit is not bound by many dramatic physical frontiers. This means that the traveller glides effortlessly and without notice from Cavan into most of its neighbours. There is nothing but a road-sign to inform you that you have entered Co. Leitrim from Co. Cavan along the

Sligo-to-Enniskillen road; the same is true of someone travelling between Virginia and Kells and crossing from Cavan into Meath; while the sailor travelling by water on the Erne north of Belturbet enters Co. Fermanagh without any visible fanfare. Standing on the southern shores of Upper Lough MacNean can feel like being very definitely in Ireland's northwest, with the breakers of Donegal Bay not that far away, while the vicinity of Kingscourt can appear closer to the landscape of south Monaghan, Louth and even distant Armagh.

When all is said and done there is a very strong, though hard to define, sense of identity in Cavan. Some outsiders have sought to do this through crude caricature. Everyone in Ireland knows about comedian Niall Toibin's jokes at the expense of the 'mean' or 'mayn' Cavanman 'eating his dinner out of a drawer'. There is even a book of Cavanman jokes. Sadly some Cavan people do themselves a disservice by responding testily to these jibes. I have often felt that Niall Toibin must be the most unpopular man in the county and that he would do well to have a police escort were he to enter here! Cavan people forget that every country has its misers who are the butt of the same jokes – the Scots in the UK, the Catalans in Spain, the Auvergnats in France etc. As a Cavan person I know of fellow inhabitants of the county who continually display unbelievable generosity.

Cavan people are no 'meaner' than anyone else. Anyone who doubts this need only pay us a visit – though don't forget your wallet!

When viewed on a map, County Cavan can resemble a chicken-leg. Its territory extends westwards towards the Atlantic ocean in a pan-handle. Its landscape, history and culture are separate from the rest of the county, seeming to belong to Ireland's north-west. This is very much a land of mountains, blanket-bogs and small lakes, populated by people who, over the generations have dedicated themselves to the heroic struggle of trying to eke a living from handkerchief-sized holdings of indifferent size. Yet this has often incited tremendous resourcefulness in its people, who developed the practice of digging holes in the bog, which were then filled in with a mixture of lime and sods taken from the higher mountain slopes.

Archaeologists believe that the first inhabitants to people Co. Cavan arrived in the Blacklion area perhaps six thousand years ago and the many prehistoric buildings testify to how long this region has been inhabited. Blacklion was also the first port-of-call of the fungal spores of the potato blight when it entered Cavan in 1845. The vicinity of Blacklion is easily penetrated from both east and west, but much of west Cavan remained isolated and cut off from the outside world until the twentieth century. This was the last part of the county in which Irish was spoken. Isolated it may have been, but the poverty of the soils compelled many people to leave in search of livelihoods in the wider world.

The quiet village of Glangevlin lies near to The Shannon Pot, source of Ireland's longest river. It is also near to the border between the Irish Republic and Northern Ireland, however a border ran along here long before man appeared on the scene. There's a natural watershed here and it is not uncommon for springs to arise within a hundred metres of each other but take divergent routes; one flowing into the Shannon, the other goes northwards, ending up in the river Erne.

The View from Brackley Lake

This prehistoric burial site high on the slopes of the Cuilcagh mountains dates from around four thousand years ago in the early Bronze Age when the climate was substantially different to our day. At the time the uplands had a more equitable and drier climate than the wetter areas lower down which were useless for agriculture; so naturally the higher slopes of Cavan's mountains were preferred both by the living and the dead.

The Giant's Grave is indeed a grave, though its eventual inhabitant was unlikely to have been huge. Archaeologists call these grave types portal tombs. They were originally covered by a mound of stones and earth, but this has long since disappeared.

Local folklore has an interesting story about the people buried here. The story goes that two giants met and began challenging each other from either side of a deep valley. The first giant was goaded into jumping over the cleft (ever since known as The Giant's Leap), which he did without difficulty, whereupon he was challenged to jump over it backwards. This was beyond his gymnastic abilities and he came crashing down on the valley floor, resisting all attempts at resuscitation. He was then buried in the eponymous Giant's Grave. His no doubt long-suffering wife was buried in a smaller tomb nearby, christened the Giantess's Grave, while a yet smaller portal tomb earned the appellation of the Baby Giant's Grave.

The Giant's Grave,
Burren

Bellavally or Glan Gap is the only communications route between the panhandle of Cavan and the rest of the county. It was excavated thousands of years ago by ice, but legend has a more picturesque version. The wise blacksmith called An Gobán Saor lived on the slopes of Slieve Anierin to the south, along with a huge cow noted for her superabundant milk. One day she moved off to the north, yet the size of her distended udder was so large that it gouged out Bellavally Gap as she walked over the ground.

At the far east of the gap is a glacial erratic, or stone which was carried a great distance by the ice before being unceremoniously dumped. For generations this has been called Maguire's Chair, and on a clear day it is possible to see the spire of Cavan's Catholic Cathedral from here.

The valley is largely uninhabited – its slopes nowadays covered by tree plantations; the only living souls are sheep, housed at night in sheep-folds whose illuminations can strike terror into the uninitiated when seen from afar. Their regularly-spaced lamps seem to belong to recently-landed Unidentified Flying Objects.

At the west end of the valley is the small hamlet of Glangevlin. This area was one of the last in which Irish was spoken in Co. Cavan and in the 1920s attempts were made to establish a Gaeltacht (or designated area for Irish speakers) here.

Life has always been a struggle for Glangevlin's inhabitants, and substantial emigration has been a fact of life. In other respects fortune was less harsh here. The Great Famine (1845-7), so destructive of human life in neighbouring parishes, hardly touched Glangevlin, and refugees seeking food came here from great distances.

The inhabitants' good fortune owed to their isolation and resourcefulness; they ate what they could grow themselves, and even spun coarse linen from home-grown flax.

Sweat houses were a common feature of the upland areas of West Cavan. A fire was lit inside these dry-stone structures and the heat produced was used by bathers to relieve a variety of skin complaints.

Bellavally Gap, Burren

People approaching Swanlinbar on a clear day will notice a curious-shaped mountain. This is Ben Aughlin, known locally as the Ben Mountain. Its odd shape is due to the erosive power of millennia of streams and rainwater. In the past, young people from the surrounding area climbed this mountain on important feast days in the folk calendar like Derenach or Bilberry Sunday, (usually the last Sunday in July), to indulge in trials of strength like tug o' war, as well as other types of youthful horse-play.

The Ben Mountain lies just to the north of the border in Co. Fermanagh. Whenever a rock-slide occurred on its slopes it was interpreted as an ill omen for Fermanagh and its people.

Swanlinbar allegedly takes its name from three mining developers who founded the town – Messrs Swann, Linn and Barr. Each man wanted to name the town in his honour. A compromise was found: the town was named after all three.

A more accurate account of where the name comes from is contained in the name used by generations of Cavan people for the town – Swad. This implies that it took its name from a stream or srath in Irish.

The town of Swanlinbar has a long and colourful history. In the eighteenth century it was the location of a thriving iron extraction and processing industry. The iron in the local mountains was thought to attract lightning strikes. It was smelted using charcoal from the abundant local forests. The iron ore soon ran out (as well as the forests), yet Swanlinbar was saved by its sulphurous springs where a popular spa developed. This attracted hypochondriacs who arrived feeling a little under the weather, but in many cases left seriously ill – if they left at all. Notions of hygiene were in their infancy, while standards of accommodation were so low that many opted to stay in their carriages.

Spas were a fad, and the sojourns of the Prince Regent, later King George IV, with Mrs Fitzherbert at Brighton ushered in a new taste for the health-giving properties of holidays by the sea. The fate of Swanlinbar's spa was sealed.

Ben Aughlin Mountain

The idea of linking the Shannon and Erne rivers by canal was first mooted in the 1770s. In 1838 the Irish Board of Works appointed an engineer to survey potential routes, and one from near Belturbet through Ballyconnell and Ballinamore to the Shannon in Co. Leitrim was chosen. This was to be thirty-seven miles in length and would involve construction of sixteen locks. Work began in 1846, at the height of the Great Famine. Belturbet became the workshop for the canal, with the manufacture of a plethora of equipment such as dredgers.

The estimated overall cost of construction was in excess of £228,000. It was opened in 1860 but in all the years following its buildings its waters were graced by the grand number of six commercial vessels. The age of canals in Ireland had passed: railways were already spreading their iron tentacles far and wide, even in Cavan.

The canal fell into disuse, many stretches clogged by weeds. It had helped drainage in the often water-logged fields along its length, and this had been one of the original aims of the canal. It probably deserves the unenviable accolade of the most expensive drainage ditch in European history!

The late twentieth century saw the growth of sailing as a major leisure activity, affordable to a wide spectrum beyond the super-rich. In the early 1980s a decision was taken to restore the Shannon- Erne Canal for use by cruisers and other leisure craft. Its sixteen locks were re-built, weeds and other debris were cleared and tow-paths were constructed along its length. It was formally opened in 1993 and continues to be a major contributor to tourism in the area. As it runs through both the Irish Republic and Northern Ireland it is a visible icon of co-operation between the two.

Between Ballyconnell and Ballinamore the canal flows through the area of Magh Sleact. One of the most important ritual centres of pre-Christian Ireland, it was the location of a stone idol to the god Crom. Known as the Killycluggin Stone, devotion took the form of sacrifices of the first born of every family and flock.

Shannon-Erne Canal

Killeshandra has long had a reputation of being a busy market town drawing its property from the surrounding countryside and the resilience of its inhabitants.

The town's name comes from the Irish for the church of the old ring-fort. The ancient parish church set beside the town's lake is indeed built within the ditches of a rath or ring-fort, which may have been used for religious rituals in pre-Christian times.

The first urban centre was established here in the second decade of the seventeenth century by the Craigs and Hamiltons, two Scottish planter families. The latter built a castle on the town's outskirts, named not immodestly Castlehamilton. Its lands were extensive, spreading from the town as far as Killykeen and in the mid-eighteenth century it was surrounded by elegant terraced gardens.

In the following century Castlehamilton came into the hands of a colourful landlord with political ambitions, Robert Southwell. His political ambitions could never overcome his inability to spend beyond his means, and he was forever having to dodge process-servers and others looking for their money. This led to his nick-name of "Sunday boy" Southwell, as Sunday was the only day the court officers didn't work and so it was the only day he could leave home without fear of arrest. He was eventually forced to sell up and the house and lands of Castlehamilton were bought by a Dublin business-man who just happened to be called Hamilton – no relation of the original founders.

Drummully House, now the site of the old Holy Rosary convent, just outside Killeshandra, was the location for the foundation in 1895 of the first agricultural co-operative society in Co. Cavan. The house's owner, Arthur Lough, was an associate of Count Horace Plunkett (1854-1932), father of the Irish co-operative movement. The society established auxiliary creameries throughout the county and remains a significant player in diary processing under the name Lakeland Dairies. Drummully House was taken over in the 1920s by a missionary order of nuns specialising in medical treatment. It remained the order's mother house until its closure in 1985, since when it has sadly become derelict.

The Church of the Rath, Killeshandra

JIM McPARTLIN

rva sits peacefully and quietly amidst lakes and low-lying hills. Its geographical location is unsual in that it is in the province of Ulster (Cavan) but Leitrim in Connacht and Longford in Leinster are both within a few miles. Its placid environment seems to belie its origins; the word Arva apparently comes from an Irish word for a battlefield!

It hasn't always been inviting to visitors. At the time of the first Ulster Plantation in 1610 the lands here were granted to a Scotsman, John Browne. He came over to look at his new paradise but, so the story goes, left unimpressed. On the way back he met a Scottish friend, Claude Acheson and told him of his disappointment at the lands allotted to him. The canny Acheson asked Browne to name his price for the property at Arva. "A fast horse to take me to the nearest port for Scotland," Browne replied. Acheson just happened to have such a horse… Acheson's descendants became earls of Gosford in 1795, and developed a small town here, building a market-house between 1817 and 1837. The Achesons' fondness for gambling eventually forced them to sell up all their Irish holdings in the 1870s.

Arva was only one of the Achesons' holdings in Ireland, but compared to their other lands it was definitely the black sheep in their property portfolio. The soil was poor and output low. It was badly hit by the decline of the domestic linen industry after 1825 but worse was to come during the Great Famine. In 1847 locals were disturbed by the yelping of a dog in the town's centre which, on closer examination, proved to be some of Arva's canine population feeding on the corpse of a young woman.

According to local folklore Fleming's Folly in Ballinagh was built by a local landlord so that he could see the ship carrying his son back from America. As the nearest ocean is over eighty kilometres away he would have needed very keen sight!

Arva

Most of Co. Cavan, along with the northern portion of Co. Leitrim, as well as parishes in counties Fermanagh and Meath lie in the diocese of Kilmore. Both the Roman Catholic and Anglican dioceses have the same boundary.

This is based on a medieval territorial diocese, which was the same as the lands controlled by the rulers of Breifne, called the diocese of Tir Brun. The first cathedral may have been a few miles away on Trinity island in Lough Erne. In 1451 the parish church at Kilmore was elevated to the status of a cathedral.

The patron saint of both the church and diocese is the somewhat shadowy St Feidlimidh, or Felim, who may have been a Christianised pagan idol.

In the seventeenth century a new cathedral was built on the site by the learned bishop William Bedell who completed the translation of the Bible into Irish. Bishop Bedell is buried in the grounds of the modern cathedral, while the earlier cathedral is still used as a parish hall. A sycamore reputedly planted by the bishop also stands opposite the gateway.

The present building dates from 1864. It is both the cathedral of the Anglican diocese of Kilmore as well as being the parish church for the surrounding area. It is dedicated to the memory of bishop Bedell, and the cathedral has an original copy of his Irish bible. Its doorway is a fine example of Irish Romanesque art and it was inserted into the newly built Kilmore cathedral in 1864 when it was removed from its original site on nearby Trinity Island.

The cathedral's setting amidst tall trees and well-tended lawns is truly romantic, never more so than when the numerous birds and crows sing in their wondrously dissonant a capella chorus.

Kilmore Cathedral

Killykeen Forest Park runs along the banks of Lower Lough Erne between Cavan town and Killeshandra. It is dominated by tall conifers and provides a home to hosts of species, including squirrels and badgers. Visitors can penetrate its sylvan splendour by footpaths and nature trails and those not satisfied with a short visit can prolong their stay in one of the chalets that have been erected along its banks. Angling, especially for coarse fish like perch, is also available.

It is hard to realise that Killykeen Forest Park is largely a man-made creation. The trees may seem as old as time, but they are not part of the canopy which once girded so much of Ireland. The oldest trees here were planted as recently as three centuries ago.

Humans have lived here for millennia. There is a crannog or artificial island visible between the shores from the wooden bridge. The lands on the east side of this bridge were part of the extensive lands of the Farnhams of Farnham House, while those to the west belonged to the estate of Castlehamilton at Killeshandra. In the eighteenth century a summer house was built overlooking Clough Oughter Castle, while towards the end of the following century Somerset Maxwell, the eighth earl of Farnham built a charming cottage decorated with shells for his wife.

Killykeen is a wonderful place at any time of the day and in any season of the year. Its high stands of timber, with the gentle murmurs of the nearby lake broken only by birdsong or the occasional hopping of a fish can appear to be more fitting in Scandinavia than Ireland.

Killykeen Cottage

Clough Oughter is now no more than a gaunt ruin, the silence of its location broken only by an occasional flock of birds or the sound of a boat's outboard motor. Yet it has seen its share of noise.

A castle was first built here in the early thirteenth century by the Anglo-Norman de Lacy family. Their ambitions put them at loggerheads with the English king Henry III who recruited their rivals amongst the Gaelic Irish to clip their wings. One family more than happy to oblige was the O'Reillys who had held power in Cavan prior to the Anglo-Normans' arrival. In 1226 a royal army wrested the castle from the de Lacys' grasp and gave it back 'temporarily' to the O'Reillys, who saw the gift as permanent. Although the O'Reillys remained in control here for centuries they never lived here; instead it was used as a prison.

During the Ulster Rebellion of 1641 the castle was pressed into service as a garrison – its earlier role as a prison was not forgotten and one involuntary guest was the Protestant bishop of Kilmore, William Bedell. His imprisonment here was brief, but it did nothing for his health and he died only a few weeks after being set free in a prisoner exchange. The rebels' military leader, Owen roe O'Neill, is reputed to have died in the castle in November 1649, but it is more likely he died in a cottage on the lakeshore nearby. In 1653 Clough Oughter was the site of the rebels' last stand against the forces of Oliver Cromwell. Its location on a small island in the lake gave it some strategic advantages but a well-directed cannon-ball blew most of the south wall into oblivion, accounting for the castle's present ruinous state.

When looking at Clough Oughter Castle it should be borne in mind that the water level was once much higher.

Clough Oughter Castle

According to a long-related story, Farnham owes its name to one man's attempt to persuade a suspicious spouse to join him in Ireland. The wife of one of the early planters in the second quarter of the seventeenth century proved so recalcitrant that he changed the area's name to Farnham, supposedly because his wife hailed from the town in Surrey. She was however not convinced. Actually the name comes from the Irish *fearnain,* meaning a place where alder-trees grow, and this name was shown on a map made in the year before the first Ulster plantations.

The lands later came into the hands of the Maxwells, originally from the Glasgow area. They made it the centre of a growing mini-empire and when they were raised to the Irish peerage they adopted the title Barons Farnham.

They built an imposing edifice, partly the work of architect Francis Johnson who was responsible for Westport House amongst others. Farnham House was surrounded by splendid gardens, with a startling new innovation – heated greenhouses – added in the early nineteenth century. Many of these were sadly destroyed on January 6th, 1839 – the 'Night of the Big Wind'.

The Farnhams were non absentees who took a close (some might say too close) interest in the lives of their tenants. They employed 'moral agents' to police the behaviour of their tenants, forbade cock-fighting and provided depots throughout their lands to supply blankets and bibles – though at a heavily subsidised price.

Although the Farnhams held on to their lands longer than other landlords, the Farnham estate had been reduced to a mere fraction of its former extent by the 1930s. At the end of the twentieth century the last baron Farnham was compelled to sell Farnham House. It has since become a luxury hotel, part of the Radisson-SAS group, and is soon to be surrounded by its own golf course.

Most of the surrounding lands are still marked by a sense of order unusual in Irish landscapes. This is perhaps a relic of the long influence of the Farnhams.

Farnham House

Cavan has been the cathedral town of the Roman Catholic diocese of Kilmore since 1843. Before that the church nearest to where the bishop of the day resided had the *de facto* status of a cathedral. For many years this role was played by a small church in Cootehill. In the 1830s the bishop of Kilmore, Wexford-man James Brown, decided that his diocese needed a cathedral and that it would be built in the largest town in the diocese. The first cathedral was a relatively plain and nondescript building, eventually demolished and reconstructed in Ballyhaise, where it still serves as the local parish church.

In 1919 it was decided that a new, bigger cathedral was needed in Cavan town. The site of the town's old gaol was originally chosen, but it was found to be too restricted and so the new cathedral was built not far from where the old cathedral had stood. A design for a neo-Gothic basilica by Dublin architect Ralph Byrne was chosen. The foundation stone was laid in 1938, but work was delayed by the outbreak of World War II. Nevertheless, it was formally consecrated in 1942 and finally completed five years' later. A fair amount of diplomatic arm-twisting had to take place so as to allow the various pieces of Carrara marble to come from Italy at the height of the hostilities. These are combined with various pieces of Irish marbles of differing hues, especially in the cathedral's pillars.

There were many people who were shocked by the scale of the building. When compared to other cathedrals in Ireland, dating from the previous century, it is truly massive. It was constructed at a time when the haemorrhage of emigration left few families in the diocese unaffected.

The cathedral's spire can be seen for many miles, while the building itself seems somewhat brighter than the rest of Cavan's architecture. Its cavernous and often gloomy interior is richly adorned with different colours of limestone and marble. The Stations of the Cross are the work of Monaghan-born artist George Colley. In the 1990s the diocese of Kilmore purchased some stained glass windows by noted artist Harry Clarke (1889-1931). For many years these stood in a Dublin convent which was to be demolished.

Cavan Cathedral

The building's huge dimensions make it suitable as a venue for concerts of church music. In recent years the church's organ has been found to be suffering the affects of ageing and there are plans to replace it with a state-of-the-art instrument.

The crypt and immediate grounds of the cathedral are the burial places of numerous Roman Catholic bishops of the diocese of Kilmore, including the recently deceased Dr Francis McKiernan.

These austere and institutional buildings are the home of St Patrick's College, the largest post-primary school in Co. Cavan and the Roman Catholic diocesan college of Kilmore.

Most of the central parts of the school were built in the early 1870s to a design by Cavan-born architect William Hague junior (1836-1899). His father, also called William, was the building contractor and relations between him and the then Catholic bishop of Kilmore, Nicholas Conaty, were anything but cordial. Bishop Conaty had initially intended that the college should be nothing less than a minor seminary for the training of priests. However his ambitions were too grandiose and instead it has had to make do with educating generations of local boys (and some from overseas), many of whom have earned plaudits as players of Gaelic games.

The college has remained very close to Conaty's Episcopal successors, whose residence lies beside it from where they are able to keep an admonitory eye on teachers and students alike, while the main corridor is embellished with their portraits. However, the influence of the Catholic Church has waned even here and recently the college appointed its first lay principal.

In the past few decades the college has expanded with new sporting facilities, as well as a new IT room. Its extensive parklands have some wonderful views of the countryside surrounding Cavan town and are a haven for the region's fauna and flora.

St Patrick's College, Cavan

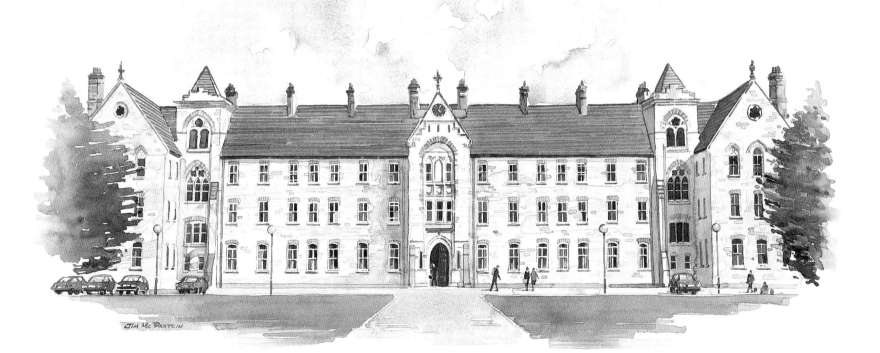

Jim Mc Partlin

The Farnhams, whose family name was Maxwell, came to Ireland from the neighbourhood of Glasgow in the early seventeenth century. Robert Maxwell was the successor of William Bedell as Bishop of Kilmore. By means of acquisitions they became the largest landlords in Cavan, but also held lands in Co. Wexford. They were elevated to the Irish peerage in 1759 as Barons Farnham, taking the title from their estate on the outskirts of Cavan town, of which they were also the landlords. They took a very close interest in the town's development and appearance. In the second decade of the nineteenth century they laid out a wide tree-lined thoroughfare for the passage of coaches through the town towards Ireland's northwest. A comfortable hotel for travellers (the original Farnham Arms) was built, while a pleasant public garden was established on the other side of the street.

The new Farnham Street was soon lined with imposing buildings such as a new Parish Church, as well as for places of Roman Catholic, Presbyterian and Methodist worship. In 1825 a new courthouse and seat of local government was built on the street's western side, in addition to fine and commodious residences for the town's 'Nobility and Gentry' and professional people.

The street is still known as Farnham Street despite having been officially renamed in honour of Sir Roger Casement in 1922. Over the years it has lost a lot of its character as Cavan's most imposing street. The park was gradually eroded by housing development and most modern travellers have neither the time or the inclination to savour its fading glory as they race along it by car.

The Library, Farnham Street

Cavan takes its name from the Irish *cabhán,* a hollow surrounded by low hills. One of these is Tullymongan, known as the Gallows Hill for the past two and a half centuries, because the town's place of execution stood here.

In the late thirteenth century the most powerful Gaelic family, the O'Reillys, chose the hill as their residence. A stone tower which was built in the mid fifteenth century was demolished around 1700.

In the later middle ages a small town existed at Cavan. This was one of the oldest urban centres in north or west of Ireland. It grew up around a small market, patronised by merchants from as far afield as Dublin and Drogheda.

The site of the first market was at the top of modern Bridge Street. It continued to be used as the site of the twice-yearly hiring fairs until the early 1950s, where young boys and girls presented themselves for hire as agricultural labourers or domestic servants. In 1825 a new market complete with a market house was built by the local landlords, the Farnhams, at the present-day Market Square. This is now occupied by the town's post office. Markets and fairs continued to be held here for a variety of products until the late twentieth century.

When counties were established as administrative units it was natural that the surrounding area would be called after Cavan and that the town would become the seat of local government, a position it holds to this day. In the 1820s the town became the cathedral site of the Roman Catholic diocese of Kilmore.

Cavan has always relied on its administrative position to provide employment, but there have also been numerous industries processing local produce like bacon. In the past decade the town's population has exploded and this has been reflected by a rash of new housing and commercial developments that have spilled out into the surrounding countryside.

Cavan Town from Gallows Hill

The tower of Cavan's Franciscan friary, also known as St Mary's Abbey, is the oldest surviving building in the town. It stands now in a small park, though until the late 1980s it was almost smothered in a jungle of nettles.

The friary was founded in 1300 by the ruler of eastern Breifne (modern Cavan), Giolla Iosa rue O'Reilly, who had moved his power-base to nearby Tullymongan Hill. The abbey provided the last resting place for many of the O'Reilly rulers, as well as a place of political asylum for deposed rulers. The church, complete with its tower, is shown on the earliest map of Cavan town, drawn circa 1590.

With the extinction of O'Reilly power and the advent of the Plantation of Ulster the friary became Cavan town's Protestant parish church. In the aftermath of the Ulster Rebellion of 1641 the planters were expelled and the church was again used for Roman Catholic worship. Owen roe O'Neill, the military leader of the rebellion, was reputedly buried here following his death at Clough Oughter Castle in 1649, though many local traditions pin-point his burial at other locations, such as Trinity Island in Lough Oughter.

Following the rebellion's suppression the church once again became a place of Protestant worship, a position it held until the opening of a new parish church on Cavan's Farnham Street in 1815. Through all this time its grounds received the bodies of Cavan people of all denominations, including the earliest Lords Farnham.

Franciscan Friary, Cavan

The stone circle atop Shantemon Hill, five kilometres north of Cavan, has traditionally been called 'Finn McCool's Fingers', because the stumps bore a resemblance in popular imagination to the fingertips of the giant of Irish mythology.

They are nevertheless very old, dating from maybe four thousand years ago. Their purpose remains unclear, though it is thought that they may represent an early form of calendar. When the sun was visible at a certain spot relative to one of the stones this could have been a cue for an important ritual or maybe even something as mundane as the planting of crops.

Nearby are the remains of the few vitrified forts to survive in Ireland. This is a little younger than the stones, (dating from between 100 BC – 100 AD) but it's even more of a puzzle. It was made by stones being heated to such an incredibly high temperature that they melted. Archaeologists are at a loss to know why this was done. It certainly didn't make the stones stronger.

In the later Middle Ages the stone circle was used by the most prominent local family, the O'Reillys, as an inauguration site. It was chosen because it was near to their residence on Cavan's Tullymongan Hill. It also gave a great view over the surrounding countryside – inauguration ceremonies were often visited by uninvited guests, intent on spoiling the party!

They were usually followed by a rowdy feast with much consumption of alcohol and food.

In the twentieth century the panorama has been somewhat spoiled by the planting of trees. However, access has been immensely improved.

Shantemon Stone Circle

Drumlane Abbey's ruins sit with quiet dignity within a landscape of silvery lakes and green-brown hills. The first monastery was founded here by St Mogue or Mo Aedh óg (my young Hugh) – also known as St Aidan in the diocese of Ferns in Ireland's south-east – in the sixth century. Mogue brought the Gospel to the area and baptised the local ruler Aodh finn, ancestor of all subsequent kings of the area.

In the twelfth century the monks here joined the Augustinian order. A local family, the O'Farrellys, claimed they were descended of St Mogue and adopted the title of coarb (Irish *comharba* or successor). They managed the church buildings and lands and were powerful voices in local church affairs. In fact, their voices were too powerful and they earned the bitter resentment of the O'Reilly clan, chieftains of East Breifne (modern Cavan). In the mid fifteenth century it was decided that the local diocese and its bishops needed a permanent base. Drumlane should have been chosen, but the O'Reillys objected. Instead Kilmore, where the O'Reillys had far more clout, was chosen.

Drumlane was a centre of pilgrimage; the pilgrims paid for the church's nave and the rebuilding of the round tower. Different building techniques were used for the base and the rest of the tower and a local tradition ascribes this to the work of two different builders – a man and a woman. But instead the differences were the work of builders – no doubt all men –

working in different periods. The bottom was probably built in the twelfth century and the top in the fifteenth.

After the sixteenth century Reformation the church was used for Protestant religious services until the early nineteenth century, while the adjacent graveyard was a place for local people of all faiths until the early 1900s.

Drumlane Abbey

Belturbet has a very strategic location. Whoever controlled this crossing of the River Erne gains access not only to the lands further west, but mastery of the Erne as it flows northwards into Fermanagh.

This was realised as early as the thirteenth century when some Anglo-Norman adventurers built a fort on Turbot Island, just to the south of the modern bridge. It was constructed on a man-made mound, but as it was made of wood has long since disappeared.

Cavan was chosen as the site of a town during the first Ulster Plantation. The man given responsibility for its development was Lancastrian native Stephen Butler. It had the right to return two members to the Irish parliament. Lying on the coach-road from Dublin to Fermanagh and Donegal, it became a transport hub for products like timber and fish. It experienced some shocking acts of violence during the Ulster rebellion of 1641, but it soon regained its earlier vigour. A bridge was built in the town over the Erne in the 1830s.

A military barracks was established near The Lawn in 1814, though there had been a barracks in the town since the 1660s. It contained billets for men as well as a cavalry school. Although closed in 1922, some of the buildings survive.

A distillery once stood in Belturbet. There have been numerous attempts to start small industry in the town, such as shoe-making, but tourism is perhaps the greatest contributor to the local economy, especially after the restoration of the Shannon-Erne Canal with its terminus in Belturbet. Each August the town hosts the Festival of the Erne, with concerts, a beauty pageant and a host of other activities.

Belturbet sits easily with its natural setting; for example, a gravelled pathway has been developed around the remains of the motte and bailey on Turbot Island, as well as along the bed of the disused narrow-gauge railway. These meet at the old railway bridge over the river from where there are spectacular views both up and down-stream.

During its hey-day Belturbet railway station (now a conference centre) was an important communications centre, with separate platforms for two different railway companies.

Belturbet

The Annalee is one of the Erne's longest tributaries. In the late eighteenth century it gave rise to a mini industrial revolution in Cavan, as mills for grinding corn and processing flax were established along its banks at various locations. One was built at Ballyhaise.

The first village was founded here during the first Ulster Plantation. In the 1730s an imposing villa was built nearby designed by German-born architect Richard Cassels (also responsible for Dublin's Iveagh House and Powerscourt House). Its interior contains an oval-shaped office, predating by many decades the more famous oval office in the White House, which it certainly influenced. The house was surrounded by terraced gardens sweeping down to the banks of the Annalee.

In the 1890s Ballyhaise House played host to Elizabeth, the estranged empress of Austria-Hungary who stayed here during one of her many peregrinations around Europe. Certain security measures were installed which can still be seen today, including thick cast-iron shutters. These renovations bankrupted the then landlord. Since 1907 this has been the location of an agricultural college which has remained an important provider of employment.

The town still houses a small central square, around which it developed. It lay on the original route from Cavan to Cootehill, and the bridge over the Annalee was originally built as long ago as 1706. An eighteenth-century landlord (and early ecologist) left instructions in his last will and testament that for every tree cut down on his estate, ten new ones were to be planted. Many of these are still to be seen on Ballyhaise's outskirts.

Ballyhaise's riverbank setting, surrounded by mature woods, makes it a very desirable place to live. For many years it has been a dormitory town of Cavan, but in the past decade its population has grown enormously, providing a home for those prepared to make an even longer commute to work.

The Annalee River at Ballyhaise

Cootehill has always been a market town. It was founded in the early eighteenth century by the Coote family, one of the largest landholders in the county.

The entrance to the wooded Bellamont demesne, home to the Cootes, lies at the end of Cootehill's main street. Bellamont House was designed in the Paladian style in the 1730s by Captain Edward Lovell Pierce, the architect of the Irish Houses of Parliament (now the Bank of Ireland) in Dublin.

The new town soon became associated with the growing trade in linen, made from flax and manufactured into cloth on local farms. This was then sold to textile buyers from the north east of Ireland who worked it up into clothes, table-cloths and sails for ships. By the end of the eighteenth century Cootehill had become one of the largest linen markets in south Ulster.

Its inhabitants reflected a wide kaleidoscope of religious beliefs. In addition to Roman Catholics, Anglicans and Presbyterians there were Methodists, Quakers and members of the Moravian Brethren or Unitas Fratrum; each with their own church. A visitor to the town in 1809 remarked upon the plethora of church spires, but remarked caustically that he had heard the abundance of places of worship did not translate into the behaviour of its inhabitants!

The decline in domestic linen manufacturing following on from greater mechanisation in the industry caused a decline in the town's market, but it nevertheless retained its vitality and reputation for raucous behaviour. In the early 1840s this attracted the attention of Fr Theobald Mathew, the Capuchin apostle of Temperance who attempted to wean Irish men and women from their attachment to drink. Prior to his arrival he received threats, ostensibly from local Orangemen, warning him that if he attempted to preach his message of sobriety in Cootehill he would not leave alive. Undaunted, Fr Matthew visited Cootehill and was met by large and enthusiastic crowds. After his departure it was revealed that the author of the threats was a Catholic publican.

In the twentieth century Cootehill maintained its vivacity. A new secondary school was opened, as well as a manufacturing facility by the Abbott corporation. The town has a lively arts scene, hosting a well-attended Arts festival each October.

Court cairns were a common form of Bronze-age burial and at Cohaw near Cootehill there are two single cairns placed back-to-back which were excavated in 1949.

Cootehill

Shercock straddles the road between Cootehill and Kingscourt, but it's older than both towns. It sits right in the middle of the 'Basket of Eggs' topography of Cavan's Drumlin country. Over the past few years actors from all over Ireland have travelled this road to attend the amateur drama festival held here each March.

No one knows where the name Shercock comes from. One not very plausible suggestion is that it comes from the Irish *sear cog,* signifying young love, a suggestion which has coined quite a few ribald jokes over the years.

The village was founded in the early seventeenth century by planters from central Scotland. It soon became prosperous, especially after the take-off of the domestic linen industry. The raw material, flax, grew very well in the local drumlin soils. Through a very complicated process it could be turned into linen fibres, which, in turn, could be made into linen cloth using weaving machines in private houses. The cloth was then bleached and sold to merchants at markets such as Cootehill. Rural dwellers could make money from weaving alone, so many farmers turned their backs on farming, often being satisfied with holdings of only a few acres. But in 1825 a factory opened in Belfast where the whole linen-weaving process was mechanised and linen cloth could be made quicker and more cheaply. The linen weavers of Cavan, and much of south Ulster, were left destitute with only their vastly reduced holdings to fall back upon.

Behind Shercock lies the brooding expanse of Lough Sillane. Legend tells that it was formed when a heedless young girl who had been sent out for water forgot to put the lid back on the well. It looks pretty but in places it is very deep, as was discovered by a local school-teacher who in July 1878 brought sixteen of his pupils, all girls, for a boating excursion. Alas the whole boat was overturned, and all aboard were drowned.

Lough Sillane

Kingscourt lies in a charming spot on the banks of the Cabra River. It is the easternmost of Cavan's towns and its proximity to counties Meath, Monaghan and Louth sets it somewhat apart. In religious terms the town and surrounding area belong to the diocese of Meath. It looks outward towards the north and east and Slieve Gullion in southern Armagh is clearly visible from elevated parts of the town. However, it most certainly belongs in County Cavan, a fact emphasised by its Gaelic football team which has won nine county championships.

It is an archetypal landlord town, with a wide main street lined with houses, shops and pubs. The landed proprietors were the Pratts, who eventually established their residence at nearby Cormy, now Cabra Castle, in the early nineteenth century. A charter granting rights to hold fairs and markets was granted in 1761 and Kingscourt made the most of its position on one of Ireland's coach-roads.

Gatherings here were not always peaceful, and in July 1814 there was a serious affray causing injury and loss of life. In August 1830 this was overshadowed by the bloodshed at the fair of Muff, some three miles to the southwest.

Built between 1869 and 1877, the town's Roman Catholic Church which occupies a site high above the town was the work of Cavan-born architect William Hague. It contains some fine stained glass by twentieth-century artist Evie Hone (1894-1955).

In recent years Kingscourt has attracted industries like brick-making and the extraction of gypsum, while its relative proximity to Dublin and the east coast has made it into something of a dormitory town for commuters. Between 1875 and 1947 Kingscourt was joined to Navan and Kells by a regular rail passenger route. While passenger services were discontinued the line was used by occasional freight trains.

It was the last town in Co. Cavan to be joined to the national rail network, as the line was closed down only as recently as 2000. The rail line is still there, and there are hopes that a rail link between Kingscourt and Navan may be re-established.

Thatched Pub in Kingscourt

Dun An Ri Forest park is probably one of Cavan's best kept secrets. It is a truly romantic place, offering visitors not only woodlands but gorges cut by fast-flowing streams, vistas as far as the Mourne mountains, as well as enchanting gardens. The park also contains the site of the village of Cabra, an urban centre beside a mill which was superseded by Kingscourt in the eighteenth century.

The land became the demesne of the Pratts (who later founded the town of Kingscourt) in 1699. There are some unusual buildings dating from the time when they were lords of the manor including an ice-house for keeping perishable foods cool in pre-refrigeration days and a militia fort. In the late 1790s nearby Kingscourt was a hotbed of activity by the rebels of the United Irishmen. A small company of local militia were raised to meet this threat.

The Cabra River is crossed by a number of small stone bridges. One of them is known as Cromwell's Bridge, though it is uncertain if the Lord Protector ever visited the area. Another, without parapets, is called Sarah's Bridge. Local folklore tells how this was named after a local woman who had received the attentions of a man for over four decades until one day he proposed to her on the bridge. The poor woman was so shocked that she fell over the side of the bridge to a watery grave.

The park also contains a wishing well, immortalised in a song promising all visitors that they would come again to Dun An Ri.

Nearby Cabra (originally Cormy) was rebuilt in the mid nineteenth century in the fashionable Scottish Baronial style by local landlord Joseph Pratt. Since the late 1960s it has been a very comfortable hotel, with an adjacent golf-course.

Cromwell's Bridge,
Dun An Ri Forest Park

Bailieborough was founded in the 1610s by William Bailie, a planter from Ayrshire in Scotland. Presbyterian settlers were attracted to the area – and until recently the town had two Presbyterian churches. In the following century the surrounding area became a centre for flax cultivation and domestic linen manufacture. Bailieborough grew up on one of the roads leading from Cavan to Belfast. The town's position as an important market-place was recognised by the construction of a market house in 1818. In the late eighteenth century it was influenced by revolutionary ideas associated with the Society of United Irishmen. A 'tree of liberty' was erected here in the 1790s and in August 1798 there was a violent confrontation between rebel sympathisers and the British army on the outskirts of the town at a location still known as The Rebel Hill. Many Presbyterian settlers subsequently emigrated to the United States. Amongst them was one William James, who eventually became one of the richest men in New York. His grandsons included the famous novelist Henry James (1843-1916) and William James (1842-1910) the philosopher and psychologist.

In 1814 Bailieborough was acquired by Col. William Young who had made his fortune in the East India Company. His son, Sir John Young, was a leading liberal politician and for a time Irish chief secretary before embarking on a career as a colonial administrator in Canada and Australia.

He lived at Bailieborough castle, now demolished. Local folklore told how one of the landlords had prohibited the cutting of even a twig in his woods on pain of death. A local lad, the only son of a widow, was seen cutting a small branch by the bailiff and was brought before the lord who ordered his hanging. The lad's mother pleaded for his life and the landlord initially relented, yet no sooner had the boy's mother left the castle than he went back on his word and had the unfortunate youth strung up. His distraught mother placed a curse on the castle, saying that no heir would ever be born there and that no nightingales would ever sing in its woods.

Bailieborough was one of the only large towns in Cavan never to have been joined to the railway network. Over the years it has housed a variety of small industries including shoe-making, a tannery, a woollens mill and an iron foundry. One of the biggest employers has been the Bailieborough Co-operative creamery.

Bailieborough Library

Mullagh is a charming village not far from the border with Co. Meath. It nestles snugly between rolling hills and the wide expanse of Mullagh Lake.

One of the oldest buildings here is Teampall Cheallaigh. These ruins date from the late middle ages and lie on the site of an even earlier church reputedly founded in the seventh century. Until the late eighteenth century this was the focus of a lively cult each July 28th in honour of St Killian, reputedly born near here. Prayers and devotion formed only a small part of the ritual and it became so rowdy that the cult was eventually suppressed by the local Catholic clergy.

St Killian was reputedly a missionary who brought the Gospel to Bavaria in the seventh century. A persistent tradition tells that he founded the city of Wurzburg. Links between Mullagh and the Bavarian city are strong, and a fine heritage centre named after the saint stands on the village's outskirts.

Teampall Cheallaigh was used for religious services until the nineteenth century. One of the rectors here William Brooke, a native of Cavan town. His son Henry Brooke (1703-1783) achieved fame and notoriety as a writer and playwright of the time. His daughter, Charlotte (c. 1740-1793) collected surviving examples of Irish epic poetry and printed them, along with translations in *The Reliques of Irish Poetry* (1789).

Without her work many of these poems would have been lost forever.

Raffony House, to the west of Mullagh village, was the birthplace of Agnes O'Farrelly (1874-1951), poet, playwright and novelist. She was professor of Irish Poetry in the National University of Ireland and was a dedicated proponent of gender equality. Mullagh was also the birthplace in 1929 of well-known actor T. P. McKenna.

Teampall Cheallaigh, Mullagh

The Moybolgue area has long been immortalised in local folklore for a confrontation between St Patrick and a shape-shifting hag which, were it not for the saint's hand and eye co-ordination, could have led to the demise of Ireland's patron saint. Local folklore tells how Patrick was travelling through Moybolgue to Ardee when he saw a beautiful girl riding on a horse being led by a handsome groom. She extended her hand to pick some bilberries growing in a nearby hedge, but no sooner had she put them to her lips than she was transformed into a vile monster or cailleach. She proceeded to eat the horse on which she had been riding (along with her groom), as well as a passing funeral cortege. It was clear that Patrick was the *plat du jour*. However, he put some stones into a sling and dispatched one into the hag's forehead, causing her to explode and fall to earth.

Moybolgue lay along the borders of Cavan and Meath. In the years following the Anglo-Norman invasion in the late twelfth century a wooden fort was built here on an earthen mound which is still visible. The nearby remains of Moybolgue church date from the later middle ages. The nave may once have had a bell-tower. Another piece of local folklore tells how, during the Cromwellian period, the bell flew from this tower through the air, pealing as it went, to warn of the approach of the Lord Protector's soldiers. After having been attacked twice the nave was re-roofed and used for Anglican Divine Service, while at the height of the Penal Laws in the eighteenth century the ruined part of the church was used by a local priest for a Latin school. One of his pupils was the young Thomas Sheridan of Quilca, father of playwright Richard Brinsley Sheridan, and close confidant of Dean Jonathan Swift.

Moybolgue Church Ruins

It is said that Cavan has a lake for every day of the year – and in a leap year people just have to dig a hole! Most of these are small, or, like Lough Erne they are joined like jewels into immense interlocking necklace. Lough Ramor is large, one of the county's biggest, extending for nearly 10 km. Unlike most of those in Cavan's lake-lands further west it drains its waters eastwards, ultimately into the river Blackwater in Co. Meath.

It takes its name from a local deity called Miramar (literally 'fat neck' in Irish) and early sources refer to it as Loch Muinreamhair (Fat neck's lake). In the Bronze Age, settlers along its southern shore in the area of Munterconnaught left tantalising decorations on standing stones. A church was built on an island in the lake in the early middle ages, but its waters also provided a marvellous refuge for early Vikings to pillage surrounding areas. Round about 1200 AD the Anglo-Normans built a small wooden fort on its south side at Knockatemple, yet this was abandoned after only a few decades. The lands around its shores saw serious fighting during the Ulster Rebellion of the mid seventeenth century, when some of the residents of the new town of Virginia abandoned their homes, throwing their valuables into its waters. In the early nineteenth century Lough Ramor was the subject of a long, costly and ultimately ridiculous legal dispute between two local landlords as to who actually owned it and its waters.

The lake, though extensive, has never presented an obstacle to residents along its shores, and a ferry across it operated from a pier at Virginia to its southern shore well into the twentieth century. Its wide expanse has attracted numerous sailors, some fortunate enough to own the finest boats. Its shores have also attracted a wide variety of birdlife. The patient angler in search of coarse fishing such as bream and roach is more than richly rewarded. Unfortunately, in common with many lakes in Cavan it has also attracted pollution, both from agricultural effluent and the discharges of industrial units along its shores. Its fauna has also been threatened by less than sensitive developments.

Lough Ramor

Virginia is one of Co. Cavan's most picturesque towns. Its main street, lined in places with trees, extends from the parish church to a bridge and old mill, while short side-streets run off in the direction of Lough Ramor.

The town shares its name with an American state: both were named after Queen Elizabeth I, 'the Virgin Queen'. It was established as part of the first Plantation of Ulster in the early seventeenth century, though the original site for the town was at Ballaghanea, a few miles south along the shores of Lough Ramor.

It was originally intended that Virginia, along with the towns of Cavan and Belturbet, would enjoy the right to return its own members to the Irish parliament. But this plan never materialised. The town's first landlords, the Plunketts or earls of Fingall, were Roman Catholics and throughout the various dynastic disputes of the seventeenth century they continually picked the wrong side. In 1750 Virginia passed into the hands of the Taylors, Lords Headfort of Co. Meath.

Virginia lay on the main coach road from Dublin through Cavan town to Ireland's north-west. In the eighteenth century it was overshadowed by Ballyjamesduff. This all changed in the 1820s when the Cavan to Dublin road was re-routed and Virginia received a new lease of commercial life.

In the late 1990s the Roman Catholic Church in the town (originally built in the 1840s in a sand quarry) was reborn as the Ramor Theatre. As a church it had excellent acoustics. At its rear is a small cemetery where the soft lapping of the nearby lake's waves can be heard.

In the recent past Virginia has, along with other towns in the east of Co. Cavan, joined Dublin city's ever expanding commuter belt.

Virginia

Black James' Town – but who was Black James? Nobody knows for certain. In the seventeenth century there was a James Ban or 'White James' O'Reilly - Black James may have been a relative. A local tradition held that the town was named after James Dough, a blacksmith who lived in the 1790s, but the name 'B. James Duff' appears on the earliest map of Cavan in 1728, some seven decades earlier.

The town grew quickly in the eighteenth century. It lay on the main coach road from Cavan to Dublin and had numerous inns for passing travellers. It had a tannery, brewery and even a small hospital. In 1795 Ballyjamesduff was attacked and much of the town set on fire. The nearby town of Ballinagh was subsequently burned in reprisal.

In the early 1820s Ballyjamesduff lost its strategic position on Cavan's transport nexus, when the local grand jury built a new road from Cavan to Virginia which bypassed Ballyjamesduff completely but went through lands owned by Robert Burrowes of Stradone and a prominent grand jury member. All subsequent roads between Cavan and Dublin have more or less followed this route. Ballyjamesduff has since been confined to a transportation back-water.

The town was immortalised in the ballad *Come Back Paddy Reilly to*

Ballyjamesduff written by W. Percy French during his time as a Public Works engineer in Co. Cavan in the late 1880s. It is not generally appreciated that the lyrics were written in reply to a bet that no words could be found to rhyme with Ballyjamesduff! Young Willy French penned the famous song, complete with directions which, if followed literally, would lead the traveller into a lake!

A convent for nuns belonging to the Order of the Poor Clares was opened here in 1869. In the 1980s this was bought by Cavan County Council. After extensive restoration work Cavan's County Museum was formally opened here by President Mary Robinson in June 1996. One of the many artefacts in the museum is an Iron Age carved head found at Corleck near Bailieborough, showing three faces, possibly representing the past, present and future.

Ballyjamesduff

Through the Ages

Cavan has been inhabited for well over eight thousand years. Cavan's earliest dwellers were nomadic, moving from place to place. The area was covered with forests at the time and these people built flimsy structures in clearings or along river banks which could be put up easily but which were never meant to last. They didn't know how to smelt metal and so left few artefacts behind them. Bones don't survive too well as they have a habit of disappearing over time in Cavan's acidic soils.

Neolithic Cavan 4000 – 2500 BC

Between five and six thousand years ago a new type of Cavan-man and woman emerged. They belonged to an age called the Neolithic by archaeologists. The climate was warmer than today and they preferred to live in the uplands which were drier than valley bottoms. They were the area's first farmers and, apart from keeping cattle and sheep, they grew some grain crops. They were also able to make simple pots. Their lives were governed by nature and the seasons, but we know very little about how they lived. We know far more about what happened to them after death and where and how they were buried. The survival of tombs of various shapes is about the only feature that has survived from this age. These were often fairly complex, consisting of one, two or more chambers buried in a mound containing the ashes of the dead. Sometimes these would open directly to the outside, as at Cohaw where there were courts or flat areas at the entrances. This has given rise to the archaeological description 'Court Cairn'. What's more at Cohaw there were no less than five tombs. At the Giant's Grave at Burren in West Cavan, there was only one tomb. It was lined by large boulders and its entrance was marked by a massive capstone, making the structure look like a door. This was a portal tomb and was probably later in date.

Apart from being burial places they may have been sites of rituals connected with ancestor worship. They were often constructed in imposing places, sometimes along natural borders, signifying control of territory. Their builders were well organised and able to put up massive structures; later inhabitants looking at these graves or megaliths (from the Greek *mega lithos* or big stone) thought they could only have been built by giants and so often named them giants' graves.

The megalith builders were replaced around 2500 BC by people who knew how to smelt metal, including copper and tin, and how to make this into a new substance: bronze. They fashioned fine pieces of jewellery from this metal, as well as weapons like spears, but these belonged to a social elite. They were also obsessed with burial and death, but the graves from this time show a preference for single burials, Cremation went out of fashion and instead corpses were interred, sometimes after all flesh had been removed, in a crouching position.

Another feature dating from this time are the standing stones and stone rows to be found in the county, such as that on Shantemon Hill near Cavan Town. These may have been early forms of calendars, helping their builders to calculate important dates in the year.

Metal-working techniques improved so that iron could be smelted. This was a relatively plentiful metal, found not only in rocky outcrops but even in nodules in bogs. Iron could be made into weapons affordable by even the most insignificant ruler and so life became much more dangerous. People put a greater premium on security and defence, living either in farms defended by ramparts on the tops of hills or on artificial islands in lakes known as crannogs. Both ring-forts and crannogs were so successful as dwellings that they were continually remodelled and remained in use for over two thousand years.

A prominent iron-age feature in Cavan's landscape is the Black Pig's Dyke which winds its way into Co. Monaghan. Legend has it that it was dug by a teacher enraged at being turned into a pig by a dissatisfied parent. It is more likely to have been a series of earth-works built to protect against cattle-rustling.

CHRISTIANITY IN CAVAN 400-1000 AD

St Mogue (c. 490-555)

Mogue's name was originally Aodh or Hugh, and Mogue came from an Irish pet-name *Mo Aedh og,* or My Young Hugh. He was born of royal parents in the vicinity of Templeport in West Cavan, was baptised somewhere in

Leinster and went to study with St David at his monastery in Wales. When he came back to Ireland he founded a church at Ferns in Co. Wexford. The patron of that diocese is still St Aidan who is the same as Cavan's Mogue. When he returned to Cavan he began to spread the Christian gospel, first baptizing the local king and then founding a monastery at Drumlane on the shores of Lough Erne. From here monks founded a monastery at Rossinver, Co. Leitrim, and it was there that Mogue died. Older people in Cavan often prayed to St Mogue, especially during violent thunderstorms.

Other saints were active beside Mogue and numerous churches and small monasteries were founded, but as these were usually built of wood they haven't survived. Some of the saints mentioned as founders of churches, or whose cults were popular in localities, may have been Christianised "pagan" idols and deities who were co-opted into the communion of saints because devotion to them was so strong.

CAVAN IN THE LATER MIDDLE AGES (C. 1000-1500)

In the early thirteenth century the Anglo-Normans (who had arrived in Ireland after 1169) tried to conquer the Cavan area, building forts and earthworks called mottes which were sometimes accompanied by a flatter bailey. A wooden tower was built on top of the motte: these naturally have long gone but the mounds and earthworks survive, as at Moybolgue, Kilmore and Belturbet. At Clough Oughter a longer-lasting stone tower was built.

It soon became clear to the Anglo-Normans that Cavan had little to offer them. The soils were too poor and wet and were useless for the manorial type of agriculture they liked. After only a few decades they turned their back on Cavan's lakes and drumlins.

In the middle ages much of Cavan belonged to the old kingdom of Breifne. Sometimes this is mistakenly described as modern counties Cavan and Leitrim, but there were areas of the south of both counties that were never in Breifne. This kingdom was originally ruled by the O'Rourkes of Leitrim, but after c. 1200 a new ruling family, the O'Reillys, emerged in the east and in the 1290s they established their seat of power on Tullymongan Hill, overlooking the modern town of Cavan. In the following decade they introduced a party of Franciscan friars to found a monastery where many of the rulers were buried. The O'Reillys remained in charge of East Breifne for the rest of the Middle Ages.

Eoghan na feasoige O'Reilly (d. 1449)

Eoghan or 'Beardy John' O'Reilly was a pioneer. He made an unsuccessful attempt to become ruler in his youth and then sought refuge in the area of Ireland still controlled by the Anglo-Normans' descendants. In 1418 he grabbed the chieftainship and, once in power, established a market at Cavan where merchants from Dublin and the east coast could buy items in short supply at home, like hides and timber. This market became permanent and a town grew up around it. Urban centres were unknown in those parts of Ireland controlled by Gaelic Irish rulers like the O'Reillys or O'Neills and so Cavan is one of the oldest towns in the northern half of Ireland. Beardy John was a pioneer in another way. He allowed his territory to be used by forgers of English coinage (also in short supply at the time) and the Dublin parliament forbade the reception and circulation of O'Reilly's money.

SOCIETY

At this time society was entirely rural. Most people lived in extended families in houses made out of wattles covered with mud. Their diet consisted of oats and dairy products. The higher echelons enjoyed slightly more comfort, sometimes inhabiting stone tower-houses, like the one that was built at Cavan town.

SIXTEENTH CENTURY CAVAN

In the sixteenth century the English Crown made great efforts to bring the whole of Ireland into political and religious submission. This included the extension of the English system of local government and the establishment of counties or shires along the English model. In 1584 the county of Cavan was formally set up in the area under the O'Reillys' rule. In the early seventeenth century the barony of Tullyhaw containing Cavan's pan-handled was added, and that is why, to this day, the county looks like a chicken-leg or lamb chop. Unfortunately some of the leaders of the O'Reillys gave their support to the rebellion launched by Hugh O'Neill of Tyrone in the 1590s, so when he was defeated their lands were confiscated by the Crown.

This ushered in the first of several plantations where Cavan's native rulers were replaced by people whom the Crown felt were more dependable. The confiscated lands were granted to settlers from England and lowland Scotland including farmers and tradesmen, as well as government functionaries and military officers. They subsequently established villages and small towns, including Killeshandra, Bailieborough and Shercock. The most important new urban foundation of the plantation era was without doubt Belturbet, which, along with Cavan town, was granted the right to send its representatives to the Irish parliament.

Bishop William Bedell (1571-1642)

The introduction of English and Scottish planters provided a practical opportunity to extend the religious reformation. Places of Roman Catholic worship were taken over, but it was difficult to recruit ministers to preach the gospel. William Bedell, a native of Essex, was a noted scholar and linguist who was appointed provost of the newly-founded Trinity College in Dublin. He became proficient in Irish and wrote a short catechism. He was then offered the Irish bishopric – actually two – the dioceses of Ardagh and Kilmore; he preferred to take the poorer diocese of Kilmore. He considered that it was absurd to preach to the Irish in English, a language they couldn't understand, so once in Cavan he completed the translation of the whole of the Bible into Irish, as well as recruiting clergymen from the ranks of the native Irish. At the outbreak of the Ulster rebellion in October 1641 he was briefly imprisoned and died near Kilmore not long after being released. His grave is in the grounds of Kilmore Cathedral.

The O'Reillys were forced onto smaller estates and they were not happy to have their wings clipped. So, they were eager participants in the rebellion of 1641. Sadly there were numerous massacres of planters, the worst of which took place at Belturbet. The Cavan area was involved in the to-ing and fro-ing of the war that followed the rebellion, much to its impoverishment. Its military leader Owen Roe O'Neill died at Clough Oughter in 1649; Cavan was one of the last areas in Ulster where the rebels held out against the forces of Oliver Cromwell.

It is perhaps remarkable that so many of the settlers who had been expelled returned to Cavan after its defeat. They were joined by new planters who helped consolidate the previously established urban centres, as well as founding new ones at places like Ballyconnell and Scrabby.

Towards the end of the seventeenth century a final attempt to re-establish the old Irish order occurred during the reign of King James II and numerous members of the O'Reillys fought in his army at the Battle of the Boyne. The Cavan area was soon wrested from the control of the king's loyalists and amongst the engagements of this war was one at Cavan town in February 1690.

EIGHTEENTH CENTURY CAVAN

In the eighteenth century Cavan's ruling elite consisted of the descendants of planters whose connections with the area were little more than a century old.

This landed aristocracy dominated local society. This included families like the Earls of Lanesborough (who owned

Belturbet), the Cootes of Bellamont and the Maxwells of Farnham, who succeeded in 1756 in climbing aboard the bandwagon of nobility when they became Barons Farnham. Increasingly they lived in fine and imposing buildings, sometimes designed by the leading architects of the day. Ballyhaise House was the work of German-born architect Richard Cassells, and Bellamont House near Cootehill was designed by the architect of Ireland's old Parliament House (now Bank of Ireland) Edward Lovett Pearce. These houses were surrounded by terraced gardens and fountains and sometimes the landscape was adorned with follies, like the one built by the Flemings near Ballinagh. The houses themselves might have been draughty, but they often used ice-houses, specially dug into banks of earth in which perishable foodstuffs were kept.

At a lower level were the houses of lesser landlords and bailiffs. These were much smaller but were built in stone and had slated roofs. The houses of the majority were simple, single-story cottages, usually with thatched roofs. The living space was sometimes shared with animals. In the parts of the county where domestic linen production became common, cottages often had extensions built on to house looms. Farm sizes were small and farming was a mixture of cereal production and livestock.

The majority of the population was Roman Catholic, and so legally excluded from sharing in the exercise of power. However the draconian Penal Laws were rarely put into practice. Nevertheless Catholic religious services had to be held in flimsy structures like barns and priests had to travel to the Continent to receive clerical education. There were numerous schools, some taught by former clerical students, who received payments of a penny a day or a few sods of turf. These were also held in flimsy buildings, though the long-held image of the 'hedge school' in the open air belongs more to romantic imagination.

There were numerous communities of Presbyterians – the descendants of Scottish planters of the previous century and also excluded politically by the Penal Laws – living in the eastern and northern parts of the county, especially around Bailieborough, Shercock and Kingscourt. John Wesley, the founder of Methodism, paid many visits to Co. Cavan and was always received by enthusiastic crowds.

Cathal bui Mac Ghioilla Ghunna (c. 1680-1756)

The majority of the population was still Irish speaking. The eclipse of the old Gaelic political order had robbed poets of their traditional patrons and forced them into a more precarious condition. Cathal, a native of the Cavan/Fermanagh border area, was compelled to work as a carter, but whatever money he made was soon spent on drink. He wandered throughout Ulster, usually moving on once he had outstayed his welcome. On one occasion he was granted a night's refuge by a Catholic priest on condition that he would move on the next day. But when he awoke the next morning he found that Cathal was indeed gone - with his horse, his best over-coat and his house-keeper!

Dr Thomas Sheridan (1687-1738)

A poet and classical scholar born in Cavan and educated in Trinity College, he set up a private school in Dublin's Capel Street which soon failed because of his lack of financial acumen. He is best known for his close friendship with Jonathan Swift who often visited him at his home at Quilca near Virginia, and helped him out on the frequent occasions he needed money. According to local folklore, Swift was introduced on one such visit to a local farmer of prodigious size named Doughty who could easily carry a horse across his shoulders. This inspired the character of Lemuel Gulliver in the land of the Lilliputians. Swift was the god-father of Thomas Sheridan's son Thomas (1719-88), who became an actor and theatre manager, and who was the father of the well-known dramatist Richard Brinsley Sheridan (1751-1816).

EXPANDING CAVAN

During the reign of Queen Anne (1702-14) Cavan, along with most of Ireland, was criss-crossed by a network of coach roads. Many of these can still be traced today. Cavan was no longer cut off from the outside world. Road-building technology was not far-enough advanced to allow roads to skirt Cavan's many hills, so instead they had to go over the top of them. As these roads were poorly maintained they were very dangerous, especially on the descent from the summit of a hill, when it was not uncommon for carriages to topple over.

A scattering of small towns and villages appeared in this century. Many were the results of landlord initiatives, eager to add the profits of a market to the money they extracted from their estates. These included Ballyhaise, Arva, Ballinagh, Kingscourt and Kilnaleck. Other villages grew up more informally around way-side inns whose names they then adopted. These included Crosskeys, on the old Cavan to Dublin road around an inn called The Crossed Keys, and Red Lion, a village in West Cavan ultimately succeeded by another leonine marketplace called Blacklion.

THE ECONOMY

The eighteenth century was a time of growing economic prosperity in the county. Most of this was creamed off by the landholding aristocracy, but some filtered down to the farmers and artisans. The agricultural sector benefitted from a new demand for livestock. Ballyjamesduff's fairs and markets were reckoned to be amongst the best in the region for black cattle. The rural sector benefitted too from the growth of flax and the production of linen on farms. Much of this was sold at local markets, of which the one at Cootehill was pre-eminent. Cootehill attracted a very heterogeneous population, including Quakers and members of the Moravian Brethren or Unitas Fratrum.

SPUDS

The potato had also begun to be cultivated widely. It proved popular because it could feed a growing population from smaller areas and still leave money for the landlords' rent. The availability of apparently inexhaustible if not very tasty food, as well as greater prosperity from processing flax into linen persuaded many small farmers that they could earn a living from ever smaller patches of ground and subdivision of holdings between sons and daughters became common. The full dangers of this policy would become clear in the middle of the following century.

MINING

Other sectors of the economy, including mining, also benefitted. Iron was extracted from the hills around Swanlinbar and smelted locally into ingots. Once these iron ore deposits were exhausted a new source of wealth was discovered in the sulphurous springs which attracted Ireland's hypochondriacs into travelling to Swanlinbar in search of cures for often nonexistent ailments.

RELIGION

As the eighteenth century drew to a close most of the anti-Catholic Penal Laws were either relaxed or removed altogether. In the 1790s a number of simple Roman Catholic churches were built such as at Kildoagh near Bawnboy, but the Catholic community was too poor to afford larger edifices.

The revolutionary ideas circling in Europe in the last decades of the century spread to Ireland and found a receptive audience especially amongst the county's Presbyterian communities in Bailieborough and Kingscourt. It was here that the United Irishmen had their greatest support. In 1798, the fateful year of rebellion, a bloody encounter took place near Bailieborough between the local United Irishmen and the British army. Some Presbyterians chose to leave Cavan for North America, including the young William James from Bailieborough, who like many Scottish-Irish immigrants became fabulously wealthy in their new home. He is better known as the grandfather of Henry and William James.

The Brookes of Rantavan

Henry Brooke was born in Mullagh around 1703. After going to Trinity College he moved briefly to London where he worked as a playwright, until one of his plays was banned. After this he returned to Rantavan near Mullagh where he continued to write poetry. He was a gifted translator and passed on an interest in Irish to his daughter Charlotte. She collected many Irish poems and epics, publishing one of the first translations of these in 1789 under the title *Reliques of Irish Poetry.* She died in poverty in 1793.

NINETEENTH CENTURY CAVAN

The advent of the Act of Union in 1801 meant very little in Cavan. Most people were engaged in what amounted to subsistence agriculture, supplemented here and there by household industry. Towns were growing and Cavan town in particular began to be surrounded by teeming suburbs of indigent refugees from the countryside who were attracted by the town's apparent prosperity. A new broad street lined by a park was laid out by the Farnhams in Cavan town. This also had a fine court house and parish church.

The seats of the landholders became more palatial, sometimes having heated glass-houses for exotic plants like orange trees. Their inhabitants were immune to the hardships of their tenants. In 1825 a factory had been established in Belfast which meant that much of the flax-processing could be done more quickly and more cheaply in a factory environment. This knocked the bottom out of the domestic linen industry, not just in Cavan but throughout the south and west of Ulster. Meanwhile the population of Cavan, buoyed on by the potato, was reaching ever more dizzying heights. The census of 1841 showed that there were a little under quarter of a million people living in the county, a figure never surpassed to this day. Many of these were living on farms of less then ten acres surviving on an unbalanced diet in which potatoes were the largest single element.

In the decades leading up to the Famine there had been a number of scares of impending trouble. In the early 1830s there had been a particularly nasty outbreak of cholera which decimated the poor of Virginia. On the evening of January 6th 1839 Cavan, along with the northern half of Ireland, was visited by a frightening hurricane. 'The Night of the Big Wind' caused relatively few human deaths, but its impact on livestock, many of which were in the open air, was terrible. Many houses in both urban and rural areas were destroyed by fire, while Lord Farnham's glass-houses were also destroyed.

NATIONAL EDUCATION

There were lots of small schools in the county, some founded by landlords or operated by clergymen. In the early nineteenth century many British-based evangelical societies established schools in Co. Cavan, but there was no universal system of education until 1831 when the British government set up a board of National Education. Groups of local people were given part of the money for building a school if they provided the land. The board then paid the teachers' salaries. The system was designed to be non-religious, but over time the 'national schools' came to be dominated by the local Roman Catholic clergy. Many of the teachers were poorly paid and poorly qualified, and often suffered from drink problems.

THE TEMPERANCE MOVEMENT

Alcohol abuse affected all sectors of society. The poorest often spent money they could ill afford on locally-produced booze, often of inferior and dangerous quality. A Capuchin friar, Fr Theobald Mathew, felt that Ireland's people could never hope to gain respect unless they gave up their drinking habits, so in 1838 he launched a national temperance movement. Huge gatherings were held, at which thou-sands 'took the pledge' to abstain from alcohol. Fr Mathew visited Cavan and held a meeting outside Butlersbridge.

NEWSPAPERS

The spread of literacy touched all, though it was only the more well-to-do who could afford to buy books and newspapers. In 1818 a local newspaper was established called the *Cavan Herald,* which ran for seven years.

Zachariah Wallace (1821-57)

A native of Dublin, Wallace helped to establish the *Anglo-Celt* newspaper in Cavan in February 1846 and in the following year became its owner and editor. Under his control the paper took a marked independent, non-confessional stance. Wallace supported greater rights for tenant farmers, as well as the introduction of secret voting. He was also a promoter of local enterprise and mining ventures. In 1853 he was imprisoned on a charge of libelling a British army regiment. Even though he spent less than a year in jail the experience broke his health and he died aged only thirty-five.

THE FAMINE

Cavan's potato crop was hit by blight in the late summer of 1845. The disease seems to have entered the county from the west: it was in Blacklion that the strange and unaccountable destruction of the potato crop was first noticed. From there the calamity spread throughout the county. Worse was to come when in the following year the potato crop was again attacked leading to massive distress. In the 1830s the British government had attempted to deal with the growing problem of Irish poverty by extending the British system of Poor Law administration to Ireland. This was based on workhouses whose grim interiors provided a modicum of support and help but whose forbidding interiors were designed to dissuade all but the most desperate from seeking assistance. Initially three workhouses were built in the county – at Cavan town, Cootehill and Bailieborough. But when mass hunger and disease struck they proved completely unequal to the challenge.

The Famine cut like a scythe through the population of Cavan's poor. Between 1841 and 1851 the county's population declined by over 28%, a trend which was to continue for a century. Far more lethal than starvation, which accounted for a minority of deaths, was the awful cocktail of diseases which were unleashed, including typhus and cholera. Those in a front-line position for dealing with the poor were at greatest risk, such as doctors and those working in the poor houses. Auxiliary fever hospitals were also set up, although some were no sooner opened than they were burned down by local residents fearing infection. For most

members of the local elites and growing middle classes the Famine was at most an inconvenience, leading to an increase in beggars in the streets.

There were some landlords whose charity and humanity stand out, including Christopher Nixon of Blacklion, John Tatlow of Kilnaleck and Pierce Morton of Kilnacrott who accelerated his descent into bankruptcy by acts of kindness to local people in the area. Other landlords, such as Lord Farnham, were unmoved by distress, and continued to evict tenants for non-payment of rent.

Some areas were hit worse than others. Mountainous Glangevlin in the county's west attracted refugees looking for food from as far away as Galway, yet the neighbouring areas of Blacklion and Doobally were devastated. People were forced to supplement their meagre food supplies with grasses and chicken-weed.

Many homes were left empty and sometimes locals peopled their shells with ghosts who did not take kindly to anyone attempting to set up house there. Some villages were also wiped off the map. Before the Famine there had been small clusters of urban life at places such as Kilgolagh and Glen in the south of the county, Ballinacargy along the Annalee and Coroneary near Bailieborough, but the depopulation of the Famine and its aftermath reduced these places to mere names. The fate of the small village of Tober in West Cavan was more dramatic. It had grown up on a spur of the Sligo-to-Enniskillen coach-road. It was also the site of religious rituals associated with a holy well – rituals which were often accompanied by more than prayers, so much so that the local parish priest suppressed the cult shortly before the Famine. Then a new road following a different route was laid down. The Famine had a devastating affect on the population, but the coup de grace came in June 1861 when a cloudburst caused a landslide and floods which buried under mud what remained of the village.

POLITICS AND SOCIETY AFTER THE FAMINE

What was most striking was how little the social structures had changed after the Famine. At the top remained the landlords. Some went bankrupt; their lands were taken over by the newly established Encumbered Estates Court and sold to the highest bidder. These were often investors with no links (and seldom any conscience either), keen to make good their investments, had even fewer problems with evicting tenants than their predecessors. Most landlords still demanded high rents to allow them to pursue the lifestyle they thought befitted members of the aristocracy. The Humphreys of Ballyhaise were amongst the worst: they were newcomers to Cavan. The family had grown rich

as wool merchants in Dublin and with their wealth had bought Ballyhaise House and estate.

In political terms the landlords still called the shots. At election time they brought those of their tenants who had a vote to the central polling stations where they were compelled to declare openly for whom they wished to vote. As their landlord had told them who to vote for it was a brave tenant who went against his landlord's declared wishes. The Humphreys, for example, always supported the most reactionary candidate. An independent-minded tenant might face immediate eviction.

The introduction of the secret ballot in 1872 proved decisive and in the following general election of 1874 two Home Rule candidates were returned to Parliament for Cavan. This was very much against the wishes of the landlords.

The Catholic Church in Cavan gained a new confidence in the years following the Great Famine. This was reflected in new church building, as well as a greater role in education and health-care. Bishop James Brown had established a new cathedral in Cavan town in 1843 but it was his successor, the autocratic Nicholas Conaty, who not only established a new diocesan seminary but introduced orders of nuns to run schools and convents.

William Hague Jnr (1836-99)

Born in Cavan town, he trained as an architect in Dublin. He was responsible for the designs of more than three dozen churches and religious institutions throughout Ireland, including the buildings of St Patrick's College, Cavan. He also designed a number of private residences. He was one of the finest and most original practitioners of the Gothic Revival spirit in Irish architecture.

Transport

In the later nineteenth century Cavan was opened up to the wider world by new transport links. First there was the canal which was built between the Shannon and the Erne, some of which passed through the county. Work was started on this less than a decade after the Famine. It was a complete failure – costing a huge amount but attracting hardly any traffic. Canals were being bypassed throughout Ireland by railways, and they soon spread to Cavan.

In 1856 the Midlands and Great Western Railway built a branch line from the Inny Junction in Co. Longford to a new railway station in Cavan town. In the following decades other railway companies built both stations and railway-lines throughout the county, for example the station at Belturbet housed platforms for two different lines using differing railway gauges. Railways allowed for the transport of goods and people; they were the places where most emigrants began their journeys into exile and so they were locations marked by harrowing scenes of grief where family members said their farewells to each other, certain that they would never see each other again. Railways also killed off a lot of small-scale local industry. In Belturbet a small distillery had been opened in the 1820s. It closed after a while but reopened amidst wild scenes of drunkenness in October 1848. However, it could not stand up to the competition of cheaper whiskies coming from outside Cavan, even though considerable amounts used to disappear at railway-stations before getting to Belturbet! Railway construction was not without its drama, with some residents vowing to prevent lines being built on their lands. There were also several accidents, mostly caused by engines running over people walking on the lines.

No trains run in Co. Cavan any more, but in some locations, such as Belturbet, station houses have been converted to other uses. A surviving stretch of railway embankment leading to a bridge over the Erne has been made into a beautiful nature walk.

Rural Life

Life for many people remained a harsh struggle for survival. The most common form of housing remained the single-storied cottage, whose space could be extended by building an extension at either side. There was usually a porch at the front. An open fire was used for both cooking and heat, and smoke was allowed to escape through a hole in the roof. The almost universal fuel was turf and the fire was never allowed to go out completely. Food was cooked in a large pot suspended by a chain over the fire. During the hours of darkness and throughout the long months of winter any non-natural lighting was provided by rush lights, or occasionally by tallow candles – bees' wax candles were reserved for the more affluent. Within this confined space it was far from uncommon to find ten, twelve, maybe more people competing for space, often packed like sardines. The roof was usually of thatch which provided an ideal form of insulation for cottages. The coat of thatch might be repaired annually, but replacement was uncommon and was left to professional thatchers who were usually small farmers themselves.

The towns of Cavan provided goods and services to the surrounding countryside. They were places whose population remained static until comparatively recently, except on market and fair days when their peace was disturbed by drinking and fighting. The line between town and country was often blurred however; many town-dwellers kept some animals, especially pigs and hens in their back yards.

Conditions for those living in towns were if anything worse than for those in the country. A report of 1868 from Cavan town pains a picture of families living in insanitary 'courts', cheek-by-jowl with open sewers, which were recognised as a happy hunting-ground for contagious diseases.

Health

Child mortality was common, but for those who fell ill there was little hope of access to professional medical help; in any case it was far away and practitioners invariably charged fees beyond the reach of most people. If they were the victims of a serious accident they might be brought to the infirmary in Cavan town or in one of the county's poor houses, but as the standards of medicine and medical care were low compared with today, such a journey was merely prolonging a life already shortened prematurely. It was probably because of this connection between poor houses and hospitals that many people in Cavan were reluctant, until as late as the 1960s, to go into hospital.

For many ailments there were cures, either herbal or possessed by an individual of the locality who had inherited it from his father. These often involved the placing of mud from a sacred site and were accompanied by prayers.

A wide spectrum of illnesses were treated by a visit to a sweat-house. These were small, stone, mortar-less structures shaped like a bee-hive. Their interiors were lined with rushes and heated by turf. After disrobing the patient crept in through a small opening which was then partially closed and sat in the vaporous atmosphere where they sweated profusely for a short period. Afterwards they emerged, hoping to find their clothes where they had left them. Sweathouses were used for arthritis, baldness, skin diseases and even for deafness. They were a common feature of the upland areas of West Cavan and neighbouring parts of Leitrim and Fermanagh.

EDUCATION

Access to schools was along mud-covered lanes and through water-logged fields, usually by pupils in bare feet. Standards of teaching varied greatly from teacher to teacher, but while the education imparted was quite basic, it was the only formal education most received, and it was found suitable in the lands far from Cavan where most of them finally settled. A problem of education in rural Cavan (and throughout rural Ireland) until the 1950s was that many students' schooling was interrupted by the demands of agricultural work. So it wasn't uncommon for children to be absent for long periods at certain times such as hay-making or lambing.

The medium of education was English and this helped to kill off the use of Irish, which had died out in most areas by 1900. In some areas of the county, such as Glangevlin in West Cavan, it remained in use for longer.

Agnes O'Farrelly (1874-1951)

A native of Cross near Mullagh, Agnes was committed to Irish studies. She was also a dedicated feminist. A novelist and poet, she attempted to found an Irish language college in Glangevlin during the 1920s and have the area proclaimed a *Breac Ghaeltacht* to preserve the use of Irish there. She succeeded Douglas Hyde as professor of Irish Poetry in the National University of Ireland.

THE SEARCH FOR WORK

Farms were too small to avail a living to more than one family member and even then this was a bitter living. After the Great Famine there were few sources of employment other than the land in Cavan. The late nineteenth century was marked by a move away from tillage in favour of dairying which needed fewer hands.

The local economy became dominated by dairying, but local farmers benefitted very little from sales of milk and butter. In order to address this Arthur Lough of Killeshandra established in 1896 a co-operative society for the processing and distribution of butter and other agricultural products. In succeeding years other co-operatives were founded throughout the county. In their early years they faced entrenched opposition from local shop-keepers and merchants and the Catholic hierarchy.

Hiring Fairs

Some young teenage men and women found temporary employment as farm labourers and domestic help with more prosperous farmers as hired help. This was done through hiring fairs held each May and November in towns like Cavan and Belturbet. Those taken on were hired for a six-month period and often had to work for fourteen hours per day, seven days a week. Some were treated fairly well, being fed and housed adequately, but young girls were sometimes the victims of sexual abuse. Hiring fairs remained a fact of Cavan life up until the 1950s.

A Military Life

Another form of employment was enlisting in the local militia. This might involve service in the regular 'line' army and quite a number of Cavanmen saw action in the Crimean War. Yet employment by the militia was never more than short-term and could never provide a proper living.

Mining

There was still some mining activity for coal around Kilnaleck and for iron ore near Redhills, but these gave very little employment and had more or less been exhausted by 1900. The various railways gave some employment too, for porters and linesmen.

Marcus Daly (1851-1900)

Born on a small farm near Ballyjamesduff, he left for America supposedly with the funds realised from selling a stolen cow. He went to California and then hit inland, where his skill as a mining engineer was legendary. He bought what appeared to be a worked-out silver mine in Anaconda, Montana. This was to prove the largest copper deposit yet discovered. Copper soon came into demand to transport electricity throughout the world and through his copper mining ventures Daly became one of the richest men in America.

Emigration

The great Famine gave impetus to mass migration from Cavan. People had been travelling from Cavan to the New World since the early seventeenth century; many young

Scottish-Irish had gone to American in the eighteenth century, in common with Presbyterians from throughout Ulster, and seasonal migration to work in Scotland and along Ireland's east coast had also occurred. In the decades leading up to the Great Famine emigration had continued at a steady rate, mainly to North America, but those leaving tended to be those already rich enough to afford the costs of travel.

Emigration was both a flight from the fear of death by starvation and disease, as well as a jump into the unknown and a search for a better life. Most, but not all, gained the first goal, but fewer attained the latter.

One way to mitigate the dangers of emigration was by 'chain migration'. An elder sibling might send the fare for their brother or sister to join them and would provide them with a support network until they could stand on their feet. As a result it wasn't uncommon to find whole neighbourhoods transplanted to the one location in America and often holding similar jobs.

Fr Matthew Gibney (1835-1925)

Matthew Gibney was born near Killeshandra and became a missionary priest in Western Australia. He carried out much charitable work, setting up schools both amongst those of Irish descent and for the area's aborigines. He eventually became Catholic bishop of Perth in 1887 and is perhaps best known for his presence at bush-ranger Ned Kelly's last stand at Glenrowan in 1880.

TRANSPORTATION

Hundreds of young men and women were transported to Australia up until transportation ended in 1868. Sometimes the nature of their crimes appear absurdly trivial, like the girl sentenced to transportation for stealing a bar of soap or the boy of fifteen found guilty of stealing turf. The minimum sentence was seven years, but few ever returned from the southern continent.

CAVAN EMBRACES MODERNITY

Gas lighting came to Cavan town as early as the 1850s. In 1912 the town's first cinema opened. Motor cars also appeared on the county's roads, but passage was slow. They tended to be affordable only by the landed aristocracy, doctors and other professionals and some Catholic priests. In 1911 the county was introduced to the age of flight when an aeroplane landed near to Cavan town's railway station.

In political terms the county was split between those seeking a restoration of an Irish parliament and those who wished for the maintenance of the union with the British

Crown. During the years of World War I many hundreds of Cavanmen joined up, but at home there was a growth in the numbers of those wanting complete independence. In June 1918 Sinn Fein leader Arthur Griffith won a by-election in East Cavan, over traditional Home Ruler J. F. O'Hanlon. The county was spared much of the bloodshed and violence of the subsequent War of Independence.

CAVAN ENTERS THE FREE STATE

Partition, when it came in 1922, was psychologically devastating. Journeys such as that between Cavan and Enniskillen, which had been mundane and uneventful, suddenly took on the nature of trips across an international boundary. Farms and parishes were divided and some roads used for decades were impassable.

There was a growing sense of intolerance in Cavan in the 1920s; some traditional expressions of unionism, such as Orange Order parades, were disrupted and, in the interests of peace and tranquillity, abandoned. The non-Catholic population began to decline, due to migration to Northern Ireland as well as emigration to England, Canada and New Zealand.

There were attacks on some landlord houses, such as the home of the Burrowes family in Stradone. The power of the landlords had been in decline since the beginning of the century, with many opting to sell their lands to their tenants. This process continued in the 1920s with compulsory purchases of estates by the Free State Land Commission.

SMUGGLING

Any barrier is a great temptation to smugglers, and the more the governments impose penalties the greater becomes the smugglers' resourcefulness, not to mention the respect in which they're held by the general public. During the years of the Economic War of the 1930s the British government imposed an import ban on Irish livestock. This caused prices to rise in Northern Ireland and spawned a brisk smuggling trade, in which cows were often made to swim across the River Erne.

THE EMERGENCY

During the years of World War II, during the so-called Emergency, Cavan was on the border between a neutral state and one of the combatants. There was the constant fear of invasion, but about the only excitement that occurred was caused by the occasional aeroplane crash. This was also the time of the tragic fire in Cavan town's convent.

Spirits were lifted by the success of the county's Gaelic footballers, who between 1933 and 1952 won five all-Ireland championships. The most memorable of these was in 1947, when the All-Ireland final was played in New York and the players returned as heroes.

The 1950s and early 1960s were years of gloom in Cavan. Emigration once again rose to alarming levels, with many of those leaving finding works on big public works projects in England. The decline in Cavan's railway network took hold, as one after the next of Cavan's lines ceased carrying passengers and then closed down permanently. About the one bright spot was the slow spread of electricity into rural areas.

Cavan Enters the Modern Age

A new sense of hope gained ascendancy in the late 1960s. The worm of emigration began to turn and the county's population started to rise for the first time in over a century. Small factories started to sprout up throughout the county. Television helped to make the world seemed less distant, while this was also the era of the show-bands, often performing in draughty marquees at carnivals, who brought some of the latest trends in rock music, albeit in a diluted form. It seemed as if the scourge of emigration which had been an accepted norm was no longer the lot faced by young people.

Emigration raised its ugly head again in the 1980s, but those affected were often the more educated. More and more young people gained tertiary education, which was no longer the privileged possession of a few.

The Troubles

Although the violence which rent Northern Ireland for over three decades did not have many manifestations in Cavan, it nevertheless seared the area's psychology. It was as if 'The Border' had fallen again across people's vistas. This time it was manned twenty-four hours a day and was observed by watch-towers. People lived in fear of events boiling over.

The Present and Future

At present Cavan (along with most of Ireland) is in the position of attracting migrants from all parts of the world. They bring a much-needed variety to local society and culture and their contribution to daily life is increasingly valued.

There is much to be positive about. Cavan was not richly endowed with traditional economic resources like mines, but one of its greatest resources was and still is its people. The other great resource it possesses is the beauty of its landscapes. While tourism is a major part of the local economy there has been an over-emphasis on a top-down approach to tourism projects.

More and more people recognise Cavan's intrinsic richness. There have been many large-scale hotel investments, often based in locations associated with the county's aristocracy, such as Farnham. There has also been an increase in the number of farmers' markets in the county, where consumers can benefit from the best local produce.

Throughout its history Co. Cavan has been a gateway, a place of transition, linking others into a stunningly differentiated tapestry of communities. But those who take the time to pause soon discover Cavan's unique but multi-layered sense of identity.

We must be careful to maintain a balance between town and country. The county's towns have always been dependant on their rural hinterlands. In the past this dependence was economic and commercial. Today the dependence is less direct but no less strong. It is psychological as the county's countryside offer opportunities for recreation of body and soul. This can take the form of the angler, sitting patiently for the one that hopefully will not get away, or the golfer whose shot does not go out-of-bounds or into the ever-present casual water! But sometimes the true sense of Cavan is best appreciated by the walker, maybe following the bleak yet spectacular Cavan Way footpath, or merely strolling at any time of year through one of the county's forest parks.

Cavan's countryside is like a finely cut gemstone, capable of reflecting light in a thousand different ways depending on the seasons and the ever-changing weather. In recent years many urban centres have become dormitory towns, where people sleep between the long commute to and from work elsewhere; yet when they wake up to the kaleidoscope of landscapes quite literally on their doorsteps, and the blend of past, present and future it represents, then they realize how fortunate they are to live in the midst of one of nature's jewel-cases.

Dear Reader

This book is from our much complimented illustrated book series which includes:-

Belfast	Blanchardstown, Castleknock and the Park
By the Lough's North Shore	Dundrum, Stillorgan & Rathfarnham
East Belfast	Blackrock, Dun Laoghaire and Dalkey
South Belfast	Bray and North Wicklow
Antrim, Town & Country	Dublin 4
North Antrim	Limerick's Glory
Across the Roe	Galway on the Bay
Inishowen	Connemara
Donegal Highlands	The Book of Clare
Donegal, South of the Gap	Kildare
Donegal Islands	Carlow
Islands of Connaught	Monaghan
Sligo	Athlone
Mayo	Cavan
North Kerry	Kilkenny
Fermanagh	Armagh
Omagh	Ring of Gullion
Cookstown	Carlingford Lough
Dundalk & North Louth	The Mournes
Drogheda & the Boyne Valley	Heart of Down
Fingal	Strangford's Shores
Dublin's North Coast	Lecale

Cottage
Publications

Cottage Publications
is an imprint of
Laurel Cottage Ltd
15 Ballyhay Road
Donaghadee, Co. Down
N. Ireland, BT21 0NG

We can also supply prints, individually signed by the artist, of the paintings featured in many of the above titles as well as many other areas of Ireland.

For details on these superb publications and to view samples of the paintings they contain, you can visit our web site **www.cottage-publications.com** or alternatively you can contact us as follows:–

For the more athletically minded our illustrated walking book series includes:–

Bernard Davey's Mourne	**Tony McAuley's Glens**
Rathlin, An Island Odyssey	**Bernard Davey's Mourne Part 2**

Telephone: +44 (0)28 9188 8033
Fax: +44 (0)28 9188 8063

We also have an exciting new range which cover rivers in Ireland and includes:–

By the Banks of the Bann	**The Liffey**
My Lagan Love	**Following the Foyle**